Dedication

To all those who ever struggled with learning a
foreign language and to Wolfgang Karfunkel

Also by Yatir Nitzany

Conversational Spanish Quick and Easy

Conversational French Quick and Easy

Conversational Italian Quick and Easy

Conversational Portuguese Quick and Easy

Conversational German Quick and Easy

Conversational Dutch Quick and Easy

Conversational Norwegian Quick and Easy

Conversational Russian Quick and Easy

Conversational Bulgarian Quick and Easy

Conversational Polish Quick and Easy

Conversational Hebrew Quick and Easy

Conversational Yiddish Quick and Easy

Conversational Armenian Quick and Easy

Conversational Arabic Quick and Easy
Egyptian Dialect

Conversational Arabic Quick and Easy
Lebanese Dialect

Conversational Arabic Quick and Easy
Emirati Dialect

Conversational Ukrainian Quick and Easy

YATIR NITZANY

Printed in the United States of America

Foreword

About Myself

For many years I struggled to learn Spanish, and I still knew no more than about twenty words. Consequently, I was extremely frustrated. One day I stumbled upon this method as I was playing around with word combinations. Suddenly, I came to the realization that every language has a certain core group of words that are most commonly used and, simply by learning them, one could gain the ability to engage in quick and easy conversational Spanish.

I discovered which words those were, and I narrowed them down to three hundred and fifty that, once memorized, one could connect and create one's own sentences. The variations were and are *infinite*! By using this incredibly simple technique, I could converse at a proficient level and speak Spanish. Within a week, I astonished my Spanish-speaking friends with my newfound ability. The next semester I registered at my university for a Spanish language course, and I applied the same principles I had learned in that class (grammar, additional vocabulary, future and past tense, etc.) to those three hundred and fifty words I already had memorized, and immediately I felt as if I had grown wings and learned how to fly.

At the end of the semester, we took a class trip to San José, Costa Rica. I was like a fish in water, while the rest of my classmates were floundering and still struggling to converse. Throughout the following months, I again applied the same principle to other languages—French, Portuguese, Italian, and Arabic, all of which I now speak proficiently, thanks to this very simple technique.

This method is by far the fastest way to master quick and easy conversational language skills. There is no other technique that compares to my concept. It is effective, it worked for me, and it will work for you. Be consistent with my program, and you too will succeed the way I and many, many others have.

Contents

INTRODUCTION TO
THE PROGRAM

People often dream about learning a foreign language, but usually they never do it. Some feel that they just won't be able to do it while others believe that they don't have the time. Whatever your reason is, it's time to set that aside. With my new method, you will have enough time, and you will not fail. You will actually learn how to speak the fundamentals of the language—fluently in as little as a few days. Of course, you won't speak perfect Ukrainian at first, but you will certainly gain significant proficiency. For example, if you travel to Ukraine, you will almost effortlessly be able engage in basic conversational communication with the locals in the present tense and you will no longer be intimidated by culture shock. It's time to relax. Learning a language is a valuable skill that connects people of multiple cultures around the world —and you now have the tools to join them.

How does my method work? I have taken twenty-seven of the most commonly used languages in the world and distilled from them the three hundred and fifty most frequently used words in any language. This process took three years of observation and research, and during that time, I determined which words I felt were most important for this method of basic conversational communication. In that time, I chose these words in such a way that they were structurally interrelated and that, when combined, form sentences. Thus, once you succeed in memorizing these words, you will be able to combine these words and form your own sentences. The words are spread over twenty pages. In fact, there are just nine basic words that will effectively build bridges, enabling you to speak in an understandable manner (please see Building Bridges). The words will also combine easily in sentences, for example, enabling you to ask simple questions, make basic statements, and obtain a rudimentary understanding of others' communications. I have also created Memorization-Made-Easy Techniques for this program in order to help with the memorization of the vocabulary. Please see Reading and Pronunciation in order to gain proficiency in the reading and pronunciation of the Ukrainian language prior to starting this program.

My book is mainly intended for basic present tense vocal communication, meaning anyone can easily use it to "get by" linguistically while visiting a foreign country without learning the entire language. With practice, you will be 100 percent understandable to native speakers, which is your aim. One disclaimer: this is not a grammar book, though it does address minute and essential grammar rules (please keep your eyes peeled for grammar footnotes at the bottom of each and every page of the program). Therefore, understanding complex sentences with obscure words in Ukrainian is beyond the scope of this book.

People who have tried this method have been successful, and by the time you finish this book, you will understand and be understood in basic conversational Ukrainian. This is the best basis to learn not only the Ukrainian language but any language. This is an entirely revolutionary, no-fail concept, and your ability to combine the pieces of the "language puzzle" together will come with great ease, especially if you use this program prior to beginning a Ukrainian class.

This is the best program that was ever designed to teach the reader how to become conversational. Other conversational programs will only teach you phrases. But this is the only program that will teach you how to create your own sentences for the purpose of becoming conversational.

THE UKRAINIAN LANGUAGE

The East Slavic language of Ukrainian has been the subject of a ban and derision by the Russians and often denied the status of a language in its own right. A quote attributed to Czar Nicholas II goes, "There is no Ukrainian language, just illiterate peasants speaking Little Russian," even though the Ukrainian and Russian lexicons differ by 38% (as opposed to 33% for Spanish and Italian). Outside of Russia, Ukrainian and Russian are accepted as two similar but different languages.

Ukrainian is the official state language of Ukraine and the Crimea, the first of two principal languages for Ukrainians, and one of three official languages for the unrecognized state of Transnistria, of which the other two are Romanian and Russian. It is also a recognized minority language in Bosnia and Herzegovina, Croatia, Czech Republic, Hungary, Moldova, Poland, Romania, Serbia, and Slovakia.

Written Ukrainian uses a variant of the Cyrillic script and there are an estimated forty-five million speakers of the language.

Historical linguists trace the origin of the Ukrainian language to the Old East Slavic, from which it split off about a thousand years ago, of the early medieval state of Kievan Rus'. After the fall of the Kievan Rus' as well as the Kingdom of Galicia–Volhynia, the language developed into a form called the Ruthenian language. The Modern Ukrainian language has been in common use since the late seventeenth century and has been associated with the establishment of the Cossack Hetmanate.

From 1804 until the Russian Revolution, the Ukrainian language was banned from schools in the Russian Empire, of which the biggest part of Ukraine (Central, Eastern, and Southern) was a part at the time. It has always maintained a sufficient base in Western Ukraine, where the language was never banned, in its folklore songs, itinerant musicians, and prominent authors.

The Ukrainian language can be mutually understood, to a degree, by those speaking Belarusian and Russian.

Spoken in: Ukraine

MEMORIZATION MADE EASY

There is no doubt the three hundred and fifty words in my program are the required essentials in order to engage in quick and easy basic conversation in any foreign language. However, some people may experience difficulty in the memorization. For this reason, I created Memorization Made Easy. This memorization technique will make this program so simple and fun that it's unbelievable! I have spread the words over the following twenty pages. Each page contains a vocabulary table of ten to fifteen words. Below every vocabulary box, sentences are composed from the words on the page that you have just studied. This aids greatly in memorization. Once you succeed in memorizing the first page, then proceed to the second page. Upon completion of the second page, go back to the first and review. Then proceed to the third page. After memorizing the third, go back to the first and second and repeat. And so on. As you continue, begin to combine words and create your own sentences in your head. Every time you proceed to the following page, you will notice words from the previous pages will be present in those simple sentences as well, because repetition is one of the most crucial aspects in learning any foreign language. Upon completion of your twenty pages, congratulations, you have absorbed the required words and gained a basic, quick-and-easy proficiency and you should now be able to create your own sentences and say anything you wish in Ukrainian. This is a crash course in conversational Ukrainian, and it works!

UKRAINIAN PRONUNCIATION

In this program, whenever encountering a *t'* at the end of verbs, pronounce it as a soft *"ts."* For example, "to buy" / *kupit'* is pronounced as "kupits" (with a soft sounding "ts").
Whenever encountering *y'y* or *u'u*, pronounce them as *"uo"* as in "buoy."

Kh—For the Ukrainian language as well as Middle Eastern languages, including Arabic, Hebrew, Farsi, Pashto, Urdu, Hindi, etc., to properly pronounce the *kh* or *ch* is essential, for example, *nacht* ("night" in German) or *Chanukah* (a Jewish holiday) or *Khaled* (a Muslim name). The best way to describe *kh* or *ch* is to say "ka" or "ha" while at the same time putting your tongue at the back of your throat and blowing air. It's pronounced similarly to the sound that you make while clearing your throat of phlegm. *Please remember this whenever you come across any word containing a *kh* in this program.

Again, this is *not* a pronunciation book. The sole purpose of this book is to provide you with the necessary skills in order to engage in fluent conversational communications. With regards to grammar and pronunciation, you are on your own!

NOTE TO THE READER

The purpose of this book is merely to enable you to communicate in Ukrainian. In the program itself (pages 16-40) you may notice that the composition of some of those sentences might sound rather clumsy. This is intentional. These sentences were formulated in a specific way to serve two purposes: to facilitate the easy memorization of the vocabulary and to teach you how to combine the words in order to form your own sentences for quick and easy communication, rather than making complete literal sense in the English language. So keep in mind that this is not a phrase book!

As the title suggests, the sole purpose of this program is for conversational use only. It is based on the mirror translation technique. These sentences, as well as the translations are not incorrect, just a little clumsy. Latin languages, Semitic languages, and Anglo-Germanic languages, as well as a few others, are compatible with the mirror translation technique.

Many users say that this method surpasses any other known language learning technique that is currently out there on the market. Just stick with the program and you will achieve wonders!

Again, I wish to stress this program is by no means, shape, or form a phrase book! The sole purpose of this book is to give you a fundamental platform to enable you to connect certain words to become conversational. Please also read the "Introduction" and the "About Me" section prior to commencing the program.

In order to succeed with my method, please start on the very first page of the program and fully master one page at a time prior to proceeding to the next. Otherwise, you will overwhelm yourself and fail. Please do not skip pages, nor start from the middle of the book.

It is a myth that certain people are born with the talent to learn a language, and this book disproves that myth. With this method, anyone can learn a foreign language as long as he or she follows these explicit directions:

* Memorize the vocabulary on each page

* Follow that memorization by using a notecard to cover the words you have just memorized and test yourself.

* Then read the sentences following that are created from the vocabulary bank that you just mastered.

* Once fully memorized, give yourself the green light to proceed to the next page.

Again, if you proceed to the following page without mastering the previous, you are guaranteed to gain nothing from this book. If you follow the prescribed steps, you will realize just how effective and simplistic this method is.

THE PROGRAM

Let's Begin! "Vocabulary"
(memorize the vocabulary)

I | I am	Ya
With you	Z toboyu
With him / with her	Z nym / Z neyu
With us	Z namy
For you	Dlya tebe / (**Plural**) dlya vas
Without him	Bez n'ogo
Without them	Bez nyh
Always	Zavzhdy
Was	Buv
This, This is	(Masc)Tsey, (fem)Tsya, (neuter)Tse, (plural)Tsi
You	(**informal**)Ty/ (**formal**)vy/ (**plural**)vy
Sometimes	Inodi
Today	S'ogodni
Are you / you are	(**informal**)Ty/ (**formal**)vy/ (**plural**)vy
Better	Krashche
These	Tsi
He / he is	Vin
She / she is	Vona
From	(from a place) Z, (from person) vid

Sentences from the vocabulary (now you can speak the sentences and connect the words)

I am with you
Ya z toboyu/ ya z vamy (plural)

This is for you
Tse dlya tebe

I am from Ukraine
Ya z Ukrajiny

Are you from Kiev?
Ty z Kyjeva?

Sometimes you are with us at the mall
Inodi ty z namy u molli

I am always with her
Ya zavzhdy z neyu

Are you without them today?
Ty bez nyh S'ogodni?

Sometimes I am with him
Inodi ya z nym

*In Ukrainian, the soft sign (apostrophe in the transcribed word) after a consonant letter makes that letter softer.

I was	Ya buv
To be	Buty
Here	Tut / os'
Same	Te same / te zh
Good/ Okay	Dobre
Day	Den'
It's / it is	(M)Tsey/(F)tsya/(N)tse/(P)tsi
And	i' (*pronounced as ee*)
Between	Mizh
Now	Zaraz / teper
Later / After	Piznishe/pislya
If	Yakshcho
Yes	Tak
Then	Potim
Tomorrow	Zavtra
Very	Duzhe
Good (person)	(M)Dobryj/(F)Dobra

Between now and later
Mizh teper i potim
If it's later, better tomorrow!
Jakshcho tse pizno, krashche zavtra!
This is also good
Tse takozh dobre
It is the same
Tse tezh-same
Yes, you are very good
Tak, ty duzhe dobryj/dobra
I was here with them
Ya buv/bula tut z nymy
The same day
Togo zh dnya

Maybe	Mozhe buty
You	Ty/Vy
Even if	Navit' yakshcho
Afterwards	Piznishe/ potim
Worse	Girshe
Where	De
Everything	(person) Vsi, (object) vse
Somewhere	Des'
What	Shcho?
Almost	Mayzhe
There	Tam

Afterwards is worse
Potim girshe
Even if I go now
Navit' yakshcho ya pidu zaraz
Where is everything?
De vse?
Maybe somewhere
Mozhe des'
Where are you?
De ty?
You and I
Ty i ya
What is this?
Shcho tse?

*In Ukrainian, whenever "what" is preceded by a noun, you say *yakyj*.
- *yakyj (m.)*
- *yaka (f.)*
- *yake (n.)*
- *yaki (p.)*

House / home	Dim
In / at	V, u / bilya
Car	Avtomobil' / mashyna
Already	Vzhe
Good morning	Dobrogo ranku
How are you?	Yak spravy?
Where are you from?	Zvidky ty?
Me	Meni
Hello / hi	Pryvit / dobrogo dnya
What is your name?	Yak tebe zvaty?
How old are you?	Skil'ky tobi rokiv?
Son	Syn
Daughter	Dochka
Your	Vash / tvij
But / however	Ale
Hard	Zhorstkyj, vazhko
Still	Dosi

She is without a car, maybe she is still at the house?
Vona bez avtomobilya, mozhe vona dosi doma?
I am already in the car with your son and daughter
Ya vzhe v mashyni z vashym synom i dochkoju
Hello, what is your name?
Pryvit, yak tebe zvaty?
How old are you?
Skil'ky tobi rokiv?
This is very hard
Tse duzhe vazhko
It's not impossible
Tse ne nemozhlyvo
Where are you from?
Zvidky ty?

*In Ukrainian, "what is your name?" is *yake tvoye imya?* Informally, this is *yak tebe zvaty?*, while formally it is *yak vas zvaty?*
*In Ukrainian, to indicate "hard" we use *zhorstkyj* or *vazhko*. *Zhorstkyj* indicates "hard" as in "a hard object" while *vazhko* indicates "hard" as in difficulty.

Thank you	Dyakuyu
For	Za
For (*a person*)	Dlya
That, that is	(M)Tsey/(F)tsya/(N)tse/(P)tsi
Time	Chas
Our	Nash
No	Ni
I am not	Ya ni/ne
Away	Daleko
Late	Pizno
Similar	Analogichnyj/ podibno
Other / Another	(M)Drugyj / (F)insha/druga
Side	Storona
Until	Doe
Yesterday	Vchora
Without us	Bez nas
Since	Z
Not	Ni
Before	Do

Thanks for anything
Dyakuyu za vse
I am not here, I am away
Ya ne tut, ya daleko
That is a similar house
Tse podibnyj dim
I am from the other side
Ya z inshoi storony
I was here last night
Ya buv tut mynuloji nochi

*In Ukrainian the article "a" doesn't exist.

I say / I am saying	Ya govoryu
What time is it?	Kotra godyna?
I want	Ya khochu
Without you	Bez tebe
Everywhere	Skriz'
I go / I am going	Ya jdu
With	Z
My	(M) Mij, (F) moya
Cousin	(M) Dvoyuridnyj brat / (F) dvoyuridna sestra
I need	Meni treba / meni potribno
Right now	Zaraz
Night / evening	Nich / vechir
To see	Bachyty
Light	Svitlo
Outside	Zovni
I must	Ya povynen
During	Protyagom
I see / I am seeing	Ya bachu
Happy	Shchaslyvyj (M), shchaslyva (F)
There	Tam

I am saying no / I say no
Ya govoryu ni
I want to see this in the day
Ya khochu bachyty tsey den'
I see this everywhere
Ya bachu tse skriz'
I am happy without my cousins here
Ya shchaslyvyj i bez moikh dvoyuridnykh brativ/sester tut
I need to be there at night
Meni treba buty tam u vecheri
I see light outside house
Ya bachu svitlo zovni/nazovni budynka
What time is it right now?
Kotra zaraz godyna?

*In Ukrainian, pronouns have different conjugations when relating to gender:
- "her": *yiyi*, his: *yogo*, its: *yogo* / he: *vin*, she: *vona*, it: *vono*, they: *vony*
- "my": *miy* (male), *moya* (female), *moye* (neutral), *moi* (plural)
- "their": *yikh* (same for male, female, formal, informal, and neutral)
- "your": *tviy* (male), *tvoya* (female), *tvoye* (neutral), *yikh* (plural)
- "your": (singular formal or plural): *vash* (male), vasha (fem), *vashe* (neuter), *vashi* (pl)
- "our": *nash* (male), *nasha* (female), *nashe* (neutral), *nashi*(plural)
Note: *Moikh* is the genitive as well as plural accusative form of the pronoun "my." This program doesn't address the nominative, accusative, genitive, dative, instrumental, and prepositional cases since, as previously stated, this isn't a grammar book.
*This isn't a phrase book! The purpose of this book is solely to provide you with the tools to create your own sentences!

Place	Mistse
Easy	Lehko
To find	Znajty
To look for /to search	Shukaty
Near / Close	Blyz'ko
To wait	Chekaty
To sell	Prodaty
To use	Vykorystovuvaty
To know	Znat'
To decide	Vyrishuvaty
Between	Mizh
Two	Dva
To	Do
That (*conjunction*)	Shcho

This place is easy to find
Tse mistse lehko znajty
I want to wait until tomorrow
Ya khochu pochekaty do zavtra
It's easy to sell this table
Tse duzhe lehko prodaty tsej stil
I want to use this
Ya khochu tse vykorystovuvaty
I want know where this house
Ya khochu znaty de tsej dim
Where is the airport?
De aeroport ?
I want to sleep
Ya khochu spaty
I need to know that everything is ok
Meni treba znaty shcho vse dobre

*In the last sentence, "that" is used as a conjunction, *shcho*.

Because	Tomu shcho / bo
To buy	Kupyty
Both	Obydva
Them / They / Their	Yikh /Vony / Yikh
Each / Every	Kozhnyj
Book	Knyga
Mine	Mij/moya/moye/moji
To understand	Zrozumity
Problem / Problems	Problema / problemy
I do / I am doing	Ya roblyu
Of	Z
To look	dyvytys' / shukaty
Myself	Sam / sama
Like this	Tak
Food	Yizha
Water	Voda
Hotel	Gotel'
I like	Meni podobayet'sya

I like this hotel
Meni podobayet'sya tsey gotel'
I want to look at the beach
Ya khochu dyvytysya na pliazh
I want to buy a bottle of water
Ya khochu kupyty sklyanku vody
I do it like this each day
Ya roblyu tse tak kozhnogo dnya
That is the book, and that book is mine
To knyga, i ta knyga moya
I need to understand the problem
Meni potribno zrozumity problemu
From the hotel I have a view of the city
Z gotelyu ya mayu vyd na misto
I can work today
Ya mozhu pratsyuvaty syogodni
I do my homework
Ya roblyu svoyu domashnyu robotu

There is / There are	Ye
Family	Sim'ya
Parents	Bat'ky
Why	Chomu
To say	Skazaty
Something	Shchos'
To go	Jty'
Ready	Gotovo
Soon	Skoro
To work	Pratsyuvaty
Who	Khto
Important	Vazhlyvo

I like to be at home with my parents
Meni podobayet'sya buty doma z moimy bat'kamy
I want to know why I must say something important
Ya khochu znaty chomu ya povynen skazaty shchos' vazhlyve
I am there with him
Ya tam z nym
I am busy, but I need to be ready soon
Ya zanyatyj, ale ya povynen buty gotovyj skoro
I like to work
Meni podobayet'sya pratsyuvaty
Who is there?
Khto tam?
I want to know if they are here, because I want to go outside
Ya khochu znaty yakshcho vony tut, tomu-shcho ya khochu vyjty na zovni
There are seven dolls
Ye sim lyalyok

I love	Ya kokhaju
How much	Skil'ky koshtuye
To take	Vzyaty
With me	Zi mnoyu
Instead	Zamist'
Only	Til'ky
When	Koly
I can / Can I	Ya mozhu / Chy ya mozhu?
Or	Chy
Were	Buly
Without me	Bez mene
Fast	Shvydko
Slow	Povil'no
Cold	Kholodno
Inside	Vseredyni/v/u
To eat	Yisty
Hot	Haryachyj
To Drive	Vodyty'

How much money do I need to take?
Skil'ky hroshej meni treba vzyaty?
Only when you can
Til'ky koly ty mozhesh
They were without me yesterday
Vony buly bez mene vchora
I need to drive the car very fast or very slowly
Meni potribno vodyty mashynu duzhe shvydko chy duzhe povil'no
It is cold in the library
Kholodno v bibliotetsi
Yes, I like to eat this hot
Tak, meni podobayet'sya yisty tse haryachym

World	Svit
To answer	Vidpovisty
To fly	Litaty
Yours	Tvoye
To travel	Navchytysya
To learn	Na'u'chit'sya
Children	Dity
To swim	Plavaty'
To practice	Praktykuvaty
To play	Graty
To leave	Zalyshyty
Many/much/a lot	Bagato
I go to	Ya jdu do
First	Pershyj
Time / Times	Raz

I need to answer many questions
Meni treba vidpovisty na bagato pytan'
I want to fly today
Ya khochu litaty syogodni
I need to learn to swim
Meni potribno navchytysya plavaty
I want to leave this here for you, when I go to travel the world
Ya khochu zalyshyty tse tut dlya vas/tebe, koly ya poyidu
podorozhuwaty po svitu
Since the first time
Z pershogo razu
The children are yours
Tvoyi dity
I need the books
Meni potribni knygy

*With the knowledge you've gained so far, now try to create your own
sentences!

26

Nobody	Nikhto
Against	Proty
Us / we	Nam / my
To visit	Vidvidaty
Mom / Mother	Mama
To give	Davaty
Which	Yakyj
To meet	Zustrity
Someone	Khtos'
Just	Til'ky
To walk	Khodyty
Around	Navkolo
Family	Sim'ya
Than	Nizh
Nothing	Nichogo
Week	Nedilya

Something is better than nothing
Shchos' krashche nizh nichogo
I am against him
Ya proty nyogo
We go each week to visit my family
My yizdymo kozhnu nedilyu vidvidaty moyu rodynu
I need to give you something
Meni potribno daty tobi shchos'
Do you want to meet someone?
Ty khochesh' zustrity kogos'?
I am here also on Wednesdays
Ya tut takozh po seredam
You do this everyday?
Ty robysh tse kozhnogo dnia?
You need to walk around the house
Ty povynen khodyty navkolo budynku

---

*In Ukrainian, *tobi / vam* are the indirect object pronouns of the pronoun "you," the person who is actually affected by the action that is being carried out. *Vam* is the formal and *tobi* is the informal variant.

I have	U mene ye/ ya mayu
Don't	Ni
Friend	Drug
To borrow	Pozychyty
To look like	Vyglyadaty yak
Grandfather	Didus'
To want	Khotity
To stay	Zalyshytysya
To continue	Prodovzhyty
Way	Shlyakh / zasib
That's why	Os' chomu
To show	Pokazaty
To prepare	Pidgotuvaty
I am not going	Ya ne idu
How	Yak

Do you want to look like Arnold?
Ty khochesh vyglyadaty yak Arnol'd?
I want to borrow this book for my grandfather
Ya khochu pozychyty tsyu knygu dlya mogo didusya
I want to drive and to continue on this way to my house
Ya khochu yikhaty i prodovzhuvaty na tsomu shlyakhu do moho budynku
I have a friend, that's why I want to stay with him in Lviv
U mene je drug, tomu ya khochu zalashytysya z nym u L'vovi
I don't want to see anyone here
Ya ne khochu nikogo bachyty tut
I need to show you how to prepare breakfast
Meni treba pokazaty vam, yak prygotuvaty snidanok
Why don't you have the book?
Chomu ty ne mayesh knygy?
I don't need the car today
Meni ne potribna syogodni mashyna

*In Ukrainian if you use a separate "why," it will be *chomu*. "That's why," transforms into *tomu*.
*In Ukrainian, *tobi / vam* are the indirect object pronouns of the pronoun "you," the person who is actually affected by the action that is being carried out. *Vam* is the formal and *tobi* is the informal variant.
*In Ukrainian, to indicate "way" we use *shlyakh* or *zasib*. *Shlyakh* indicates "road" while *zasib* indicates "method."

To remember	Zapam'yataty
Ukrainian	Ukrayins'ky
Number	Nomer
Hour	Godyna
Dark / darkness	Temno / pit'ma
About	Pro
Grandmother	Babusia
Five	P'yat'
Minute / Minutes	Khvylyna / khvylyny
More	Bil'she
To think	Dumaty
To do	Robyty
To come	Pryhodyty
To hear	Slukhaty
Last	Ostannij / mynulyj
Language	Movi / mova

I need to remember this number
Meni potribmo zapam'yataty tsey nomer
This is the last hour
Tse ostannya godyna
I want to hear my grandmother speak English today
Ya khochu pochuty yak moya babusya govoryt' na angliyskiy movi
I need to think more about this, and what to do
Meni potribno dumaty bil'she pro tse, i shcho robyty
From here to there it's five minutes
Zvidsy do tudy pyat' khvylyn

*In Ukrainian, the definition of *zvidsy* means "from here."
*In Ukrainian, *mova* is "language" in English. The terms "English" and "Ukrainian" cannot be used on their own when referring to a language. The word "language" always comes after the relevant word: "English" / *Anhliys'ka mova; "Ukrainian" / Ukrayins'ka mova.*

To leave	Pity
Again	Znovu
Ukraine	Ukrayina
To bring	Prynesty
To try	Sprobuvaty
To rent	Orenduvaty
Without her	Bez neyi
We are	My ye
To turn off	Vymknuty
To ask	Zapytaty
To stop	Zupynyty
Permission	Dozvil
Tonight	S'ohodni vvecheri

He needs to rent a house at the beach
Yomu potribno orenduvaty budynok na plyazhi
Tonight I need to turn off the lights early
Sohodni vvecheri ya povynen vymknuty svitlo rano
We want to stop here
My khochemo zupynytysya tut
We are from Ukraine
My z Ukrayiny
The same building
Ta sama budivlya
I want to ask for permission to leave
Ya khochu poprosyty dozvil pity
Can I leave?
Mozhna meni pity?

To open	Vidkryvaty
To buy	Kupuvaty
To pay	Platyty
Last	Ostann'ij
Without	Bez
Sister	Sestra
To hope	Spodivatysya
To live	Zhyty
Nice to meet you	Pryyemno poznayomytys
Name	Im'ya
Last name	Prizvyshche
To return	Povernutysya
Future	Majbutnye
Door	Dveri
Our	Nash
On	Na'
To get to know	Poznayomytysya

I need to open the door for my sister
Meni potribno vidchynyty dveri dlya moyeyi sestry
I need to buy something
Meni potribno shchos' kupyty
I want to get to know your sisters
Ya khochu poznayomytysya z tvoimy sestramy
Nice to meet you, what is your name and your last name?
Pryjemno poznayomytysya z vamy, yak vas zvaty i yake vashe prizvyshche?
To hope for the better in the future
Spodivatysya na krashche maybutnye
Why are you sad right now?
Chomu ty sumna zaraz?
Our house is on the hill
Nash budynok na pagorbi

*This *isn't* a phrase book! The purpose of this book is *solely* to provide you with the tools to create *your own* sentences!

To happen	Statysya
To order	Zamovyty
To drink	Pyty
Excuse me	Vybachte
Child	Dytyna
Woman	Zhinka
To begin / To start	Rozpochaty
To finish	Zakinchuvaty
To help	Dopomagaty
To smoke	Palyty
To love	Kokhaty
To talk / To Speak	Govoryty

This must happen today
Tse povynno statysya s'ogodni
Excuse me, my child is here as well
Vybachte, moya dytyna tezh tut
I love you
Ya tebe kokhaju
I see you
Ya tebe bachu
I need you
Ty meni potribnyj
I want to help
Ya khochu dopomogty
I don't want to smoke again
Ya ne khochu palyty znovu
I want to learn to speak Ukrainian
Ya khochu navchytysya govoryty na ukrayins'kij movi

*In Ukrainian, *tebe* is the "direct object pronoun" of the pronoun you.

To read	Chytaty
To write	Pysaty
To teach	Vchyty/navchaty
To close	Zachynyaty
To turn on	Vmykaty
To prefer	Viddavaty perevagu
To put	Poklasty
Less	Men'she
Sun	Sontse
Month	Misyats'
I talk, I speak	Ya govor'u
Exact	Tochno
To choose	Vybyraty
In order to	Shchob

I need this book, in order to learn how to read and write in Ukrainian
Meni potribna tsya knyga, shchob vyvchyty yak chytaty i pysaty
ukrayins'koyu movoyu
I want to teach in Ukraine
Ya khochu navchaty v Ukrayini
I want to close the door of the house and not to turn on the light
Ya khochu zakryty dveri budynku i ne vmykaty svitlo
I prefer to put the gift here
Ya viddayu perevahu poklasty podarunok tut
I want to pay less than you for the dinner
Ya khochu platyty men'she nizh vy za obid
I speak with the boy and the girl in Ukrainian
Ya rozmovlyayu z khlopchykom ta divchynkoyu po-ukrayinsky
I see the sun today
Ya bachu sontse syogodni
Is it possible to know the exact day?
Mozhna diznatysya tochnyj den'?

To exchange	Obminyuvaty
To call	Dzvonyty
Brother	Brat
Dad	Tato
To sit	Sydity
Together	Razom
To change	Zminyty
Of course	Zvychayno
Welcome	Laskavo prosymo
During	Pid chas
Years	Rik
Sky	Nebo
Up	Vgoru
Down	Vnyz
Sorry	Vybachte
To follow	Sliduvaty
Her	Vona
Big	Velykyj
New	Novyj
Never	Nikoly

I don't want to exchange this money at the bank
Ya ne khochu obminyuvaty groshi v banku
Today I want to call my brother and my dad
Syogodni ya khochu dzvonyty moyemu bratovi i
moyemu tatovi
**Of course I can come to the theater, and I want to sit
together with you and with your sister**
Zvychayno, ya mozhu pryjty v teatr, i ya khochu sydity
razom z toboyu i tvoyeyu sestroyu
I need to see your new house
Meni potribno pobachyty tviy novyj dim
I can see the sky from the window
Ya bachu nebo z vikna

To allow	Dozwolyaty
To believe	Viryty
Morning	Ranok
Except	Krim
To promise	Obitsyaty
Good night	Nadobranich
To recognize	Vyznaty/vpiznaty
People	Lyudy
To move	Rukhatysya
To move (to a place)	Pereselyatysya
Far	Daleko
Different	Inshyj
Man	Cholovik
To enter	Vvijty
To receive	Otrymaty'
Tonight	Vvecheri
Through	Cherez
Him / his	Vin/Yogo

I believe everything except for this
Ya viryu vsyomu krim tsyogo
They need to recognize the Ukrainian people quickly
Vony povynni shvydko vpiznaty ukraintsiv
I need to move your cat to another chair
Meni potribno perevesty vashu kishku na inshe krislo
I see the sun in the morning from the kitchen
Ya bachu sontse vrantsi z kukhni
I want his car
Ya khochu yogo mashynu

*In Ukrainian, to indicate "good night" we say *nadobranich*, however, it can also be said as *dobranich*.
*With the knowledge you've gained so far, now try to create your own sentences!

To wish	Bazhaty
Bad	Poganyj
To Get	Otrymaty'
To forget	Zabuty
Everybody / Everyone	Vsi/Kozhen
Although	Khocha
To feel	Vidchuvaty
Great	Chudovo/Velykyj
Next	Nastupnyj
To like	Podobatys'/lyubyty
In front	Poperedu
Person	Lyudyna
Behind	Za/Pozadu
Well	Dobre
Goodbye	Do pobachennya
Restaurant	Restoran
Bathroom	Vanna kimnata / tualet

I don't want to wish anything bad
Ya ne khochu bazhaty nichogo poganogo
I must forget everybody from my past
Ya povynen zabuty vsikh z mogo mynulogo
I am close to the person behind you
Ya poruch iz lyudynoyu, yaka stoyit' za vamy
I say goodbye to my friends
Ya govoryu do pobachennya moyim druzyam
In which part of the restaurant is the bathroom?
V yakij chastyni restoranu tualet?
I want a car before the next year
Ya khochu mashynu na nastupnyj rik
I like the house, however it is very small
Meni podobayetsya budynok, prote vin duzhe malenkyj

*In Ukrainian, *z kumos'* means "next to," for example, "I am next to him." While *nastupnyj* means "the following," for example "the next exit."

36

To remove	Vydalyty/znyaty
Please	Bud'laska
Beautiful	Garnyj
To lift	Pidnimaty
Include / Including	Vklyuchyty
Belong	Nalezhyt'
To hold	Trymaty
To check	Pereviryaty
Small	Malen'ka/malen'kyj
Real	Spravzhnij
Week	Tyzhden'
Size	Rozmir
Even though	Nezvazhayuchy na
Doesn't	Ni
So	Tak / otzhe
Price	Tsina

She wants to remove this door
Vona khoche znyaty tsi dveri
This doesn't belong here
Tut ne nalezhyt
I need to check again
Meni potribno pereviryty znovu
This week the weather was very beautiful
Na tsyomu tyzhni pogoda bula duzhe garna
I need to know which is the real diamond
Meni potribno znaty, yakyj diamant spravzhnij
We need to check the size of the house
Meni potribno pereviryty rozmir budynku
I can pay this although the price is expensive
Ya mozhu zaplatyty tse, khocha tsina vysoka (dorozhcha)
Is everything included in this price?
Chy vse vklyucheno v tsyu tsinu?

*In Ukrainian, both *tak* and *otzhe* are used to indicate "so". However *tak* definition of "so" is used to express cases such as "so much", or "so big." While *otzhe* definition of "so" is used to indicate "then."

BUILDING BRIDGES

In Building Bridges, we take six conjugated verbs that have been selected after studies I have conducted for several months in order to determine which verbs are most commonly conjugated, and which are then automatically followed by an infinitive verb. For example, once you know how to say, "I need," "I want," "I can," and "I like," you will be able to connect words and say almost anything you want more correctly and understandably. The following three pages contain these six conjugated verbs in first, second, third, fourth, and fifth person, as well as some sample sentences. Please master the entire program up until *here* prior to venturing onto this section.

I want	Ya khochu
I need	Meni potribno
I can	Ya mozhu
I like	Meni podobayet'sya
I go	Ya idu
I have to/ I must	Ya povynen
To have	U mene je/maty

I want to go to my apartment
Ya khochu yty do moyeyi kvartyry
I can go with you to the bus station
Ya mozhu yty z toboyu na avtovokzal
I need to walk to the museum
Meni potribno yty do muzeyu
I like the train
Meni podobayetsya poyizd
I am want to teach a class
Ya khochu navchaty klas
I have to speak to my teacher
Ya povynen rozmovlyaty z moyim vchytelem

Please master pages #16-#38, prior to attempting the following two pages!!

You want / do you want? - Ty khochesh / Ty khochesh?
He wants / does he want? -Vin khoche / Vin khoche?
She wants / does she want? - Vona khoche / Vona khoche?
We want / do we want? - My khochemo / My khochemo?
They want / do they want? - Vony khochut' / Vony khochut'?
You (plural/ formal sing) want - Vy khochete / Vy khochete?

You need / do you need? - Tobi potribno / Tobi potribno?
He needs / does he need? - Yomu potribno / Yomu potribno?
She needs / does she need? - Vona potrebuye/ Vona potrebuye?
We Need / do we need? - Nam potribno / Nam potribno?
They need / do they need? - Yim potribno / Yim potribno?
You (plural/ formal sing) need - Vam potribno/ Vam potribno?

You can / can you? - Ty mozhesh / Ty mozhesh?
He can / can he? - Vin mozhe / Vin mozhe?
She can / can she? - Vona mozhe / Vona mozhe?
We can / can we? - My mozhemo / My mozhemo?
They can / can they? - Vony mozhut' / Vony mozhut'?
You (plural/ formal sing) can - Vy mozhete / Vy mozhete?

You like / do you like? - Tobi podobaet'sya / Tobi podobaet'sya?
He likes / does he like? - Yomu podobaet'sya / Yomu podobaet'sya?
She like / does she like? - Yij podobaet'sya / Yij podobaet'sya?
We like / do we like? - Nam podobaet'sya / Nam podobaet'sya?
They like / do they like? - Yim podobaet'sya / Yim podobaet'sya?
You (plural/ formal sing) like -Vam podobaet'sya / Vam podobaet'sya?

You go / do you go? - Ty ydesh / Ty ydesh?
He goes / does he go? - Vin yde / Vin yde?
She goes / does she go? - Vona yde / Vona yde?
We go / do we go? - My ydemo / My ydemo?
They go / do they go? - Vony ydut' /Vony ydut'?
You (plural/ formal sing) go - Vy ydete / Vy ydete?

You must / do you have to - Ty povynen / Ty povynen?
He must / does he have to - Vin povynen / Vin povynen?
She must / does she have to - Vona povynna / Vona povynna?
We have / do we have to - My povynni/ My povynni?
They must / do they have to - Vony povynni / Vony povynni?
You (plural/ formal sing) must - Vy povynni / Vy povynni?

You have - Ty mayesh (or) u tebt ye
He has - Vin maye(or) u nyogo je
She has - Vona maye (or) u neyi je
We have - My mayemo (or)u nas ye
They have - Vony mayut'(or) u nych ye
You (plural) have - Vy mayete (or) u vas ye

Please master pages #16-#39, prior to attempting the following page!!

Do you want to go?
Vy khochete pity?
Does he want to fly?
Chy khoche vin litaty?
We want to swim
My khochemo plavaty
Do they want to run?
Vony khochut' bigaty?
Do you need to clean?
Ty povynen prybraty?
She needs to sing a song
Vona povynna spivaty pisnyu
We need to travel
My povynni podorozhuvaty
They don't need to fight
Vony ne povynni bytysya
You (plural) need to see the film
Vy povynni podyvytysya kino
Can you hear me?
Ty mene chuyesh?
He can dance very well
Vin mozhe tantsyuvaty duzhe dobre
We can go out tonight
My mozhemo pity s vvecheri
They can break the wood
Vony mozhut
Do you like to eat here?
Tobi podobayet

He likes to spend time here
Yomu podobayet'sya provodyty chas tut
We like to fix the house
Nam podobayet'sya remontuvaty budynok
They like to cook
Yim podobayet'sya gotuvaty
You (plural) like my house
Vam podobayet'sya mij budynok
Do you go to school today?
Ty ydesh do shkoly syogodni?
He goes fishing
Vin yde lovyty rybu
We are going to relax
My ydemo vidpochyvaty
They go to watch a film
Vony ydut' dyvytysya kino
Do you have money?
Ty mayesh groshi?
She must look outside
Vona povynna vyglyadaty nazovni
We have to sign here
My povynni pidpysaty tut
They have to send the letter
Vony povynni vidpravyty lysta
You (plural) have to order
Vy povynni zamovyty

Days of the Week

Sunday	Nedilya
Monday	Ponedilok
Tuesday	Vivtorok
Wednesday	Sereda
Thursday	Chetver
Friday	Pyatnytsya
Saturday	Subota

Seasons

Spring	Vesna
Summer	Lito
Autumn	Osin'
Winter	Zyma

Cardinal Directions

North	Pivnich
South	Pivden'
East	Skhid
West	Zakhid

Colors

Black	Chornyj
White	Bilyj
Gray	Siryj
Red	Chervonyj
Blue	Synij
Yellow	Zhovtyj
Green	Zelenyj
Orange	Oranzhevyj
Purple	Fioletovyj
Brown	Korychnevyj

Numbers

One	Odyn
Two	Dva
Three	Try
Four	Chotyry
Five	Pyat'
Six	Shist'
Seven	Sim
Eight	Visim
Nine	Devyat'
Ten	Desyat'

CONGRATULATIONS, NOW YOU ARE ON YOUR OWN!

If you merely absorb the required three hundred and fifty words in this book, you will then have acquired the basis to become conversational in Ukrainian! After memorizing these three hundred and fifty words, this conversational foundational basis that you have just gained will trigger your ability to make improvements in conversational fluency at an amazing speed! However, in order to engage in quick and easy conversational communication, you need a special type of basics, and this book will provide you with just that.

Unlike the foreign language learning systems presently used in schools and universities, along with books and programs that are available on the market today, that focus on *everything* but being conversational, *this* method's sole focus is on becoming conversational in Ukrainian as well as any other language. Once you have successfully mastered the required words in this book, there are two techniques that if combined with these essential words, can further enhance your skills and will result in you improving your proficiency tenfold. *However* , these two techniques will only succeed *if* you have completely and successfully absorbed the three hundred and fifty words. *After* you establish the basis for fluent communications by memorizing these words, you can enhance your conversational abilities even more if you use the following two techniques.

The first step is to attend a Ukrainian language class that will enable you to sharpen your grammar. You will gain additional vocabulary and learn past and present tenses, and if you apply these skills that you learn in the class, together with the three hundred and fifty words that you have previously memorized, you will be improving your conversational skills tenfold. You will notice that, conversationally, you will succeed at a much higher rate than any of your classmates. A simple second technique is to choose Ukrainian subtitles while watching a movie. If you have successfully mastered and grasped these three hundred and fifty words, then the combination of the two—those words along with the subtitles—will aid you considerably in putting all the grammar into perspective, and again, conversationally, you will improve tenfold.

Once you have established a basis of quick and easy conversation in Ukrainian with those words that you just attained, every additional word or grammar rule you pick up from there on will be gravy. And these additional words or grammar rules can be combined with the three hundred and fifty words, enriching your conversational abilities even more. Basically, after the research and studies I've conducted with my method over the years, I came to the conclusion that in order to become conversational, you first must learn the words and then learn the grammar.

The Ukrainian language is compatible with the mirror translation technique. Likewise, with this language, you can use this mirror translation technique in order to become conversational, enabling you to communicate even more effortlessly. Mirror translation is the method of translating a phrase or sentence, word for word from English to Ukrainian, by using these imperative words that you have acquired through this program (such as the sentences I used in this book. Latin languages, Middle Eastern languages, and Slavic languages, along with a few others, are also compatible with the mirror translation technique. Though you won't be speaking perfectly proper and precise Ukrainian, you will still be fully understood and, conversation-wise, be able to get by just fine.

CONCLUSION

Congratulations! You have completed all the tools needed to master the Ukrainian language, and I hope that this has been a valuable learning experience. Now you have sufficient communication skills to be confident enough to embark on a visit to Ukraine, impress your friends, and boost your resume so good luck.

This program is available in other languages as well, and it is my fervent hope that my language learning programs will be used for good, enabling people from all corners of the globe and from all cultures and religions to be able to communicate harmoniously. After memorizing the required three hundred and fifty words, please perform a daily five-minute exercise by creating sentences in your head using these words. This simple exercise will help you grasp conversational communications even more effectively. Also, once you memorize the vocabulary on each page, follow it by using a notecard to cover the words you have just memorized and test yourself and follow that by going back and using this same notecard technique on the pages you studied during the previous days. This repetition technique will assist you in mastering these words in order to provide you with the tools to create your own sentences.

Every day, use this notecard technique on the words that you have just studied.

Everything in life has a catch. The catch here is just consistency. If you just open the book, and after the first few pages of studying the program, you put it down, then you will not gain anything. However, if you consistently dedicate a half hour daily to studying, as well as reviewing what you have learned from previous days, then you will quickly realize why this method is the most effective technique ever created to become conversational in a foreign language. My technique works! For anyone who doubts this technique, all I can say is that it has worked for me and hundreds of others.

Note from the Author

Thank you for your interest in my work. I encourage you to share your overall experience of this book by posting a review. Your review can make a difference! Please feel free to describe how you benefited from my method or provide creative feedback on how I can improve this program. I am constantly seeking ways to enhance the quality of this product, based on personal testimonials and suggestions from individuals like you.

Thanks and best of luck,

Yatir Nitzany

Made in the USA
Columbia, SC
05 January 2023

75673575R00029